HOOTS!

Hoots! a wee book of classic Couthie humour

Published by doodlemacdoodle in association with Couthie

Bookspeed, 16 Salamander Yards, Edinburgh EH6 7DD
Tel: 0131 467 8100
Fax: 0131 467 8008
sales@bookspeed.com
www.bookspeed.com/doodle

Printed and bound in Poland

ISBN: 978-1-908661-02-9

Disclaimer
Every effort has been made to provide accurate information in this collection. Should there be any omissions or errors in this respect we apologise and shall be pleased to rectify these in any future edition.

HOOTS!

a wee book of classic Couthie humour

Published by doodlemacdoodle in association with Couthie

Couthie

Introduction

doodlemacdoodle is delighted to publish "Hoots! a wee book of classic Couthie humour" which ticks all our boxes in presenting the best of Scottish traditions in modern contexts.

Business in general, and publishing in particular is all about partnerships. With Hoots!, not only have we brought Couthie on board with its ever popular and hilarious images and texts, but also we have established a relationship with WaterAid by which we will donate 10p to their excellent work in southern Africa for every copy sold of this book and all our forthcoming titles.

More information can be found about both Couthie and WaterAid at the rear of this book.

Read this book. Laugh out loud and enjoy a glass of clean, clear Scottish water.

Kingsley Dawson

Did you want a double latte?

The advent of cheap European flights
introduced café culture and drinking good
coffee al fresco. Even in rainy Scotland
it became de rigueur.

Wis it a double latte ye wanted?

A night out on the booze left them feeling
a little unwell!

If you have ever been a bit pale
and off colour (peely-wally) after a
good night out, you may have had
a swallow (swally) too many.

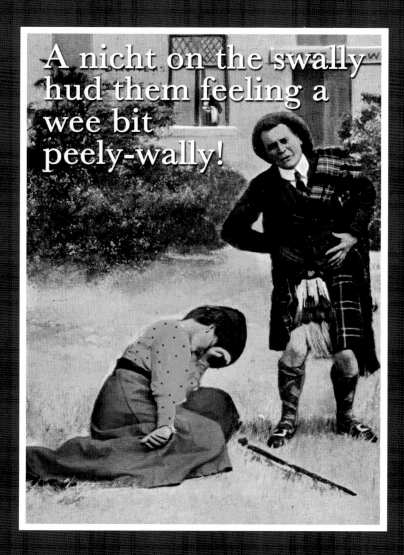

Hitch it higher Hamish or
we will never get a lift.

Hitch hiking was once more common
and comedy sketches often parodied
the cheeky methods used to get a lift.

Hitch it higher Hamish
- or we'll niver get a lift

The must have eco-friendly 'Chelsea Tractor'

All of sudden in the 1990s we went all eco-friendly, but started driving gas guzzling 4x4s for the school run.

The must have, eco friendly
'Chelsea-Tractor'

There's nothing like the seafood
and eat it diet!

Our appetite for faddy diets hasn't waned.
Here the play is on healthy 'seafood' and
'seeing food' and just wanting to eat it.

Oh God, it says here that red accessories
don't go with striped stockings!

The vagaries of fashion have perplexed
women through the ages and probably
always will.

Morag was in a daydream thinking about her wild Stitch'n Bitch nights!

Women are getting together again to re-learn how to knit, to stitch and possibly to bitch, much as they did in World War II, when the phrase was first coined.

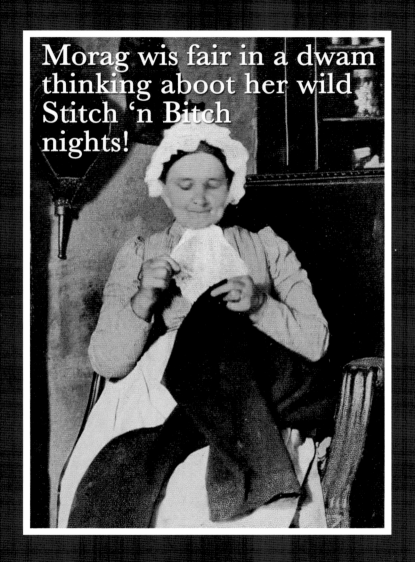

Morag wis fair in a dwam thinking aboot her wild Stitch 'n Bitch nights!

Robbie's mum always knew he
had the X Factor!

The X Factor has provided an
enduring platform for many a
mother's aspiring darlings.

Robbie's Ma
aye kent
he had the X Factor!

It's a shame men don't grow
on trees said Bella.

Dating agencies have become widely
acceptable and a vast industry has
emerged, costing hopeful singles
a pretty penny.

Tam, you can stop taking the Viagra now!

Originally developed for heart conditions,
it turned out that the little blue pills could
do much more - including producing
a large family.

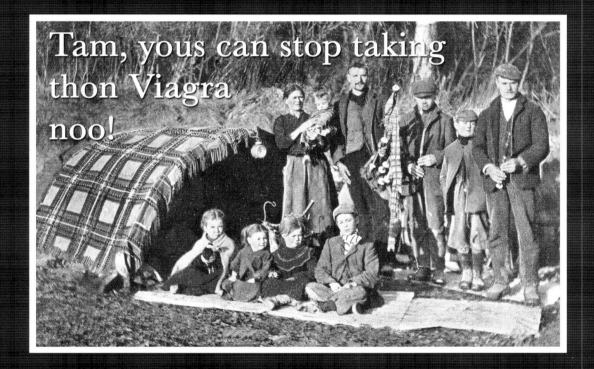

I know they are not pre-packed,
but they are definitely organic!

Earthy, organic, pesticide-free veggies often
lose out over the convenience of clean,
ready to eat, plastic wrapped options.

A ken they're no pre-packed but they're definitely organic !

Archie's first Munro was a
little disappointing.

Best to start young with the pursuit
of 'bagging' Munros (Scottish mountains
over 3,000 ft or 914m) as there are
283 challenging climbs in all.

Archie's first Munro wis a wee bit o' a disappointment

Real men love to dance!

A 'reel' is a well-known and popular
traditional Scottish country dance,
but what is a 'real man'?
The (feminist) debate rages on.

They were really looking forward
to Global Warming…

There is no denying climate change is
occurring, but it is clear this group of
women are looking forward to it.

They were all totally perplexed about
Gok's rules on how to wear stripes!

In 2006 Gok Wan shot to fame
for his pragmatic fashion advice
for women of all shapes and sizes.

They were all totally perplexed aboot Gok's rules on the wearing o'stripes!

Vivienne Westwood eat your heart out!

Vivienne Westwood transformed fashion
and contemporary culture in the 1970s
by adopting and re-interpreting
traditional tartan fabrics.

Vivienne Westwood eat yer heart oot!

Jock was not happy about
the smoking ban…

The lone smoker is now a common
feature of the Scottish streetscape,
since the introduction of the ban
on smoking in public places.

Jock wis no happy aboot the smoking ban...

Annie asked why men never do the housework…Because they're men said Daisy!

Despite the women's lib movement nothing much has changed since this image was taken. How many men do their fair share of the housework today?

Annie asked why men never do housework...

Because they're men said Daisy!

He was a bit of a wimp and totally
demoralised by her superior intelligence.

Girls are outperforming boys in all
subjects, including emotional intelligence.
Pity about the 'big jessies' still out there.

The big jessie wis fair scunnered...
He couldnae match her superior female intelligence!

The MacGregors were desperate for broadband so they could get home delivery!

With broadband internet came another innovation – home delivery. Ironically many remote communities are often better connected than some urban ones.

The MacGregors were desperate fur Broadband...

so they could hae hame delivery!

Maggie and Blackie couldn't fathom out
what their Carbon Footprint was!

Peat is still cut for fuel and to add flavour
to certain whiskies. But what on earth is
a carbon footprint and how on earth
do you measure it?

Maggie and Blackie couldnae fathom oot whit their Carbon Footprint wis!

She suspected an ulterior motive when he suggested a peep at his little shelter!

Gone are the days when a man might suggest to a woman 'come up and see my etchings'. Women today are just as likely to make the first move.

The girls were all for Solar Energy,
if only there was more sun!

The popular perception is that the sun has
to be out for solar technologies to work.
Luckily it works on cloudy days too, but it
is hard to disagree with these two ladies.

The lassies were aw fer Solar Energy....
if only there wis mair sun!

Alastair didn't have a clue about
speed dating etiquette!

By the year 2000 speed dating had really
taken off. Strict rules were necessary to
save awkwardness and embarrassment.

Alastair didne hae a scooby aboot speed dating etiquette!

Sandy was pretty foolish but he
knew how to woo a lady!

Are there really not enough good men
around that intelligent women still want
to be beguiled by charming fools?

Sandy wis awfy glaikit...
but he fair knew how tae please a lassie!

Counting units just wasn't
on Donny's radar!

Safe drinking limits have been around for
many years, yet rather few of us pay heed
or understand them. Do we even want to?

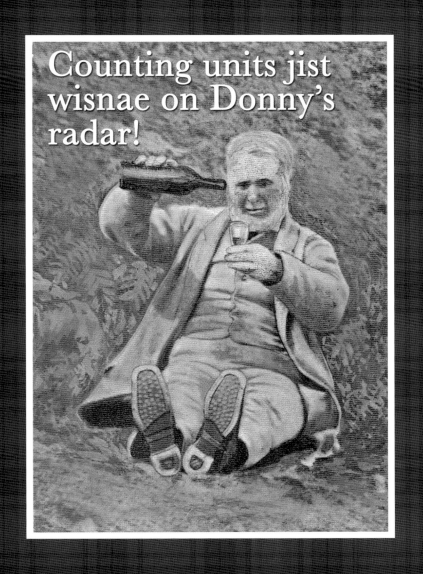

Crikey! A man at the 'call-centre' who can understand what I am saying!

A caller with a friendly Scots accent is clear and reassuring, provided they don't stray into vernacular. A lesson call centres have learnt.

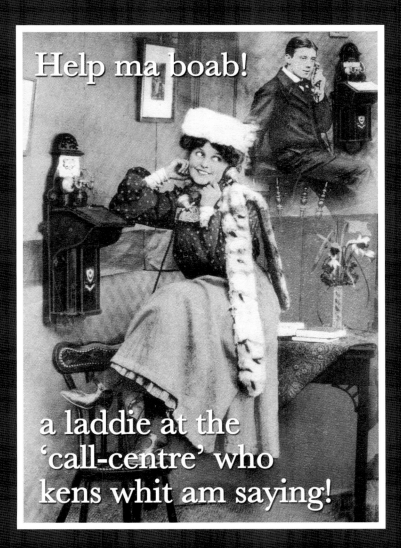

Does my bum look big in this?

Modern women remain insecure about their appearance, particularly the size of their derrières. "Insecure Woman" was a character in the British comedy The Fast Show who obsessively repeated this refrain.

About doodlemacdoodle

Building on the staggering and continuing success of our first series, 'Dynamic Words From Scotland', doodlemacdoodle will be rolling out a whole publishing programme in 2012 and beyond.

Over our 25 years of trading Bookspeed has built up a great reputation as a supplier of fabulous book ranges to retailers in town, country and tourist locations all over the UK.

We have always aimed to blend established Scottish lines with design-led gift books displaying quirky humour, bright colours and positive outlooks.

The doodlemacdoodle brand brings all these essential qualities together. It takes the most successful gift themes and formats and publishes them with modern and positive Scottish content.

This project has been initiated by Kingsley Dawson, Chairman of Bookspeed, who has recently moved desks and is enjoying being a publisher. He can be contacted via the Bookspeed office, or at doodlemacdoodle@bookspeed.biz

Och Wheesht and Get Oan Wae It

This groundbreaking Scottish addition to the Keep Calm and Carry On series provides a hilarious collection of quotes and proverbs showing Scottish wisdom at its best.

"Whit's Fur Ye'll No Go By Ye!"

Eat Haggis and Ceilidh On

Celebrating diverse Scottish delights such as; Rabbie Burns, the Auld Alliance, blazing heather, Cal Mac, flying Scotsmen, Whisky Porridge, the Gay Gordons, the mighty haggis, the Melrose Sevens, salt'n'sauce...

Braw Stuff Fae Scotland

Braw Stuff is a fascinating collection of Scottish people, ideas and discoveries from Neolithic times to the modern day including; the bicycle, the flush toilet, Clootie Wells, the Bank of England and the Ecclefechan Tart.

£4.99 (HB)
9780955264112

£4.99 (HB)
9781908661005

£4.99 (HB)
9781908661012

About Couthie

We are renowned for our ever popular and very collectable humorous cards using images from the past. These pictures were taken in the nineteenth century and we are sure all the people involved had interesting stories in their own right and no doubt deserve a book of their own someday.

Couthie also offers a wide collection of original Scottish gifts

Our latest 'Dinnae Fash Yersel' range, based on the 'Keep Calm and Carry On' theme, has taken Scotland by storm!

www.couthie.co.uk

About WaterAid

783 million people live without access to safe water and **2.5 billion people** live without access to sanitation.

1.4 million children die every year from diarrhoea caused by unclean water and poor sanitation - **4,000 child deaths a day.**

Just £15 could enable one person to access safe water, improved hygiene and sanitation.

WaterAid uses practical solutions to provide clean water, safe sanitation and hygiene education to the world's poorest people and now works in 27 countries in Africa, Asia, the Pacific region and Central America.

"I have always liked going to school even before we had the tap. Now we can enjoy washing our hands everyday which makes me feel clean and happy."

Valy Adeline, Ankafotra school, Mahaiza Province, Madagascar

10p from each copy of this book sold will be donated to WaterAid in Scotland and will go towards WaterAid's work in Southern Africa.

288701 (England and Wales) and SC039479 (Scotland)

WaterAid/Marco Betti